Savvy

FASHION ORIGAMI

ORIGAMI
ACCESSORIES
A Foldable Fashion Guide

by SOK SONG

CAPSTONE PRESS
a capstone imprint

GUIDE TO FOLDING

Making crisp, accurate creases is the key to a clean and polished origami model. Use these lines and symbols to help you and guide your creases. Don't worry if you've made a mistake or something seems confusing—just back up a couple of steps and try again.

LINES AND DASHES

 VALLEY FOLD

 MOUNTAIN FOLD

CREASE LINE

HIDDEN LINE

ACTION SYMBOLS

FOLD

PLEAT

MAGNIFIED VIEW

FOLD AND UNFOLD

REPEAT

ROTATE

UNFOLD

TURN OVER

DISTANCE

FOLD BEHIND
(MOUNTAIN FOLD)

SQUASH

FOCAL POINTS

DIFFICULTY LEVEL

EASY   MEDIUM   CHALLENGING

COMMON FOLDS

VALLEY FOLD

Fold the paper to the front so the crease is pointing away from you, like a valley.

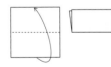

MOUNTAIN FOLD

Fold the paper to the back so the crease is pointing up at you, like a mountain.

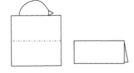

SQUASH FOLD

Open the pocket and squash down flat. Most often, this will be done on the existing pre-creases.

INSIDE REVERSE FOLD

Fold the flap or corner to the inside, reversing one of the creases.

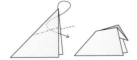

OUTSIDE REVERSE FOLD

Fold the flap or corner to the outside, reversing one of the creases.

PLEAT FOLD

Fold the paper to create a pleat.

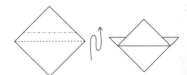

TABLE OF CONTENTS

TOTE BAG

The right bag can make a statement while still being functional. This two-toned paper **tote bag** even has a pocket to store things, which makes it a great alternative to an everyday purse—toss in all your essentials, and you're ready to go!

HOW TO USE

⊞ Fold this tote bag in a variety of colors to match your different outfits.

⊞ Try folding it with larger, heavier paper to carry around some of your lightweight belongings, like origami paper!

How To Fold

 1

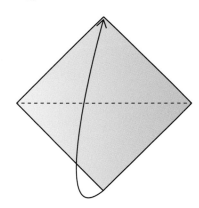

Fold the paper in half diagonally (Note: The side facing up will become the body of the tote; the side facing down will become the handle and bottom.)

2

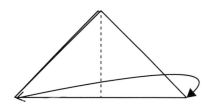

Fold the paper in half horizontally and then unfold.

3

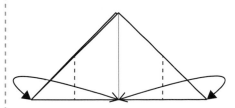

Fold both side corners into the center crease and then unfold.

 4

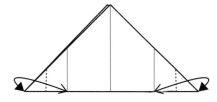

Fold the side corners into the creases made in the previous step and then unfold.

5

 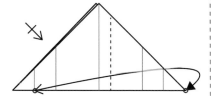

Fold the right corner to the farthest crease on the left side and then unfold. Repeat on the opposite side.

6

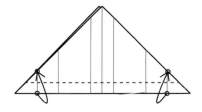

Fold the bottom edge up to the top of the creases made in step #4. Use the circled points as references.

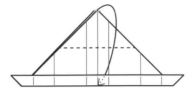

Fold the front corner flap down to the bottom and tuck it beneath the long strip from the previous step. (See the next step for reference.)

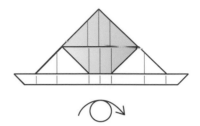

8

Turn the paper over.

Fold the top corner down to the bottom edge.

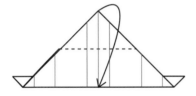

10

Fold the sides up at an angle so they line up with the creases made in step #5. (Note: The next step is a magnified view.)

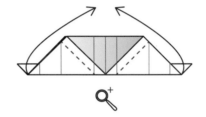

11

Fold the side corners into the outside folded edge.

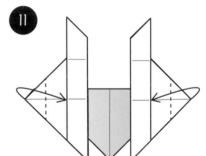

12

Fold the side flaps in and then unfold.

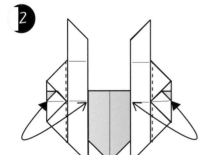

13

Tuck the side flaps inside and hide them underneath the long straps using the crease made in step #12. (See the next step for reference.)

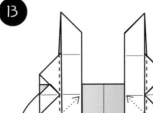

14

Turn the paper over.

15

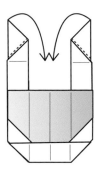

Fold the triangles at the top of the handles down.

16

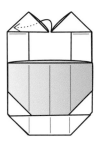

Slide one of the triangles inside the other triangle on the top. (Note: The tote section will become curved and 3-D.)

17

While holding the triangle flaps together, one inside the other, mountain fold the top corner to the back to lock the handle in place.

18

Mountain fold the corners on the top to shape the handle and create a stronger paper lock

Enjoy your finished tote bag!

SCARF

Scarves have always been a practical, yet fashionable accessory. You can tie a scarf around your neck to add a fun pop of color to an outfit. Or fold your scarf into a narrower shape, and use it to hold your hair out of your face while making a chic style statement! Try folding this paper version with different patterns, or layer multiple sheets to add more colors.

HOW TO USE

Fold using a 6- or 8-inch (15- or 20-cm) square and your paper scarf is the perfect size to wrap around a water bottle, adding some color and making it easily identifiable as your own.

It can also be used as a napkin ring or hair tie.

1

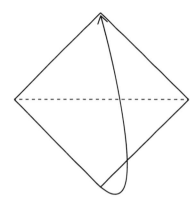

Fold the paper in half diagonally. (Note: The side facing down will become the majority of your scarf; the side facing up will become the contrasting trim.)

2

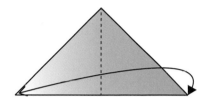

Fold the paper in half again, bringing one corner to the other corner, and then unfold.

3

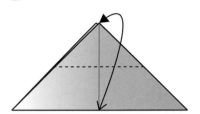

Using just the front layer of paper, fold the top corner down to the bottom edge and then unfold.

4

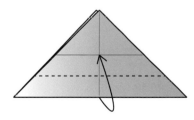

Fold the bottom edge up to the crease made in the previous step.

5

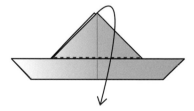

Fold the front flap down on the existing pre-crease.

6

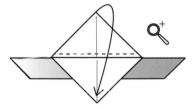

Fold the back flap down, making sure it is slightly higher than the previous flap to create a color-changed border. (See the next step—a magnified view—for reference.)

7

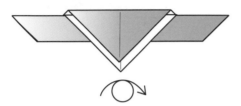

Turn the paper over.

8

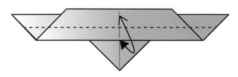

Fold the long folded edge up to the top and then unfold.

9

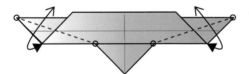

Fold a diagonal from the outside corners to where the bottom edge meets the triangle and then unfold. (Use the circled points for reference.)

10

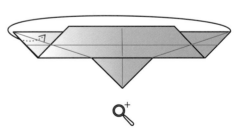

Wrap one corner around to the front and slide the tip into the opening on the opposite side. Leave a small triangle notch on the bottom. (Note: The next step is a magnified view.)

11

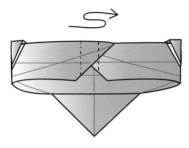

Make a small pleat in the center where the papers overlap inside.

12

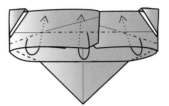

Mountain fold in on the existing pre-creases. (Note: The sides will be the angled creases from step #9 and the back edge will be a straight edge.)

13

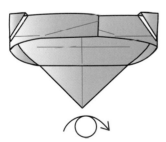

Turn the paper over.

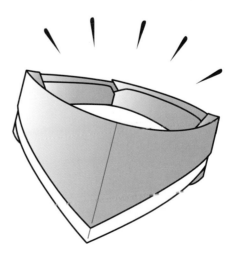

Enjoy your finished scarf!

BOW

Throughout history, **bows** have been a classic accessory for hair or clothing. The right bow can add a pop of color and surprise to an outfit or look. Try folding multiple bows in a variety of sizes and colors. You can attach these paper versions to your headbands and hairpins or to your outfit using pin-backs. You can also make this bow thinner and less bulky by using half a square of paper instead—just start from step #2.

HOW TO USE

- Add a paper bow in a sparkly pattern to a headband for some extra formal flair.

- Attach a fun paper bow to an unexpected accessory, such as a purse, clutch, or tote bag.

How To Fold

1

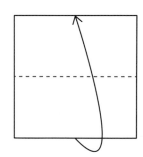

Fold the paper in half horizontally. (Note: The side facing down will become the pattern of the bow.)

2

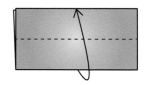

Fold the paper up and in half again.

3

Fold the paper in half vertically and then unfold.

4

Fold the sides into the center and then unfold.

5

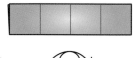

Turn the paper over.

6

Fold the right side across to the crease on the opposite side and then unfold. Repeat on the left side. (Note: The next step is a magnified view.)

7

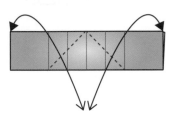

Fold the sides down diagonally along the center crease and then unfold.

8

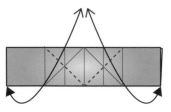

Fold the sides up diagonally along the center crease and then unfold.

9

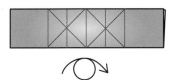

Turn the paper over.

10

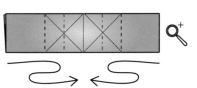

Using the existing vertical pre-creases, pleat the sides into the center. (See the next step—a magnified view—for reference.)

11

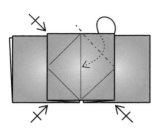

Inside reverse the upper right corner using the angled pre-creases. Repeat on all the other corners of the center square.

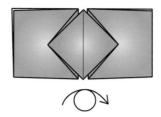

Turn the paper over.

13

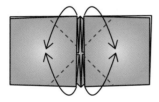

Fold the corner tips down to shape the bow. (See the next step for reference.)

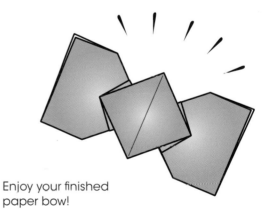

Enjoy your finished paper bow!

14

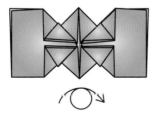

Turn the paper over.

BROOCH

Brooches and pins are decorative accessories that can change an outfit dramatically, whether it's adding a hint of color or an unexpected element. You can find pin backs and fasteners at your local craft store or online and use these paper versions as part of your everyday outfits. You can also stick them on with double-sided tape or pre-adhesive glue dots or foam squares.

HOW TO USE

- Fold this brooch in various sizes and colors to put on your jackets, scarves, and dresses.

- Make multiples and add brooches to a headband or a hairpin!

How To Fold

1

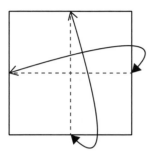

Fold the paper in half in both directions and then unfold. (Note: The side facing down will become the visible part of your brooch.)

2

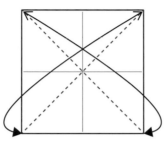

Fold the paper in half diagonally in both directions and then unfold.

3

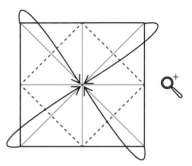

Fold all four corners into the center. (Note: The next step is a magnified view.)

4

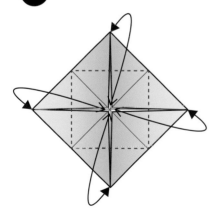

Fold all four corners into the center again and then unfold.

5

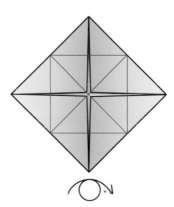

Turn the paper over.

6

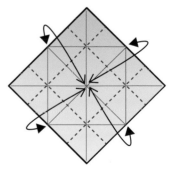

Fold the sides into the center crease, first horizontally, then vertically, and then unfold. (Note: Make sure to keep both the top and bottom layers in place.)

7

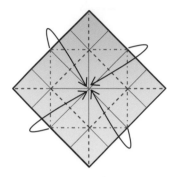

Fold all four sides of the square into the center while pinching the corners. (See the next steps for reference.)

8

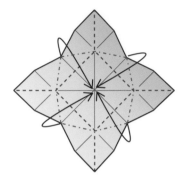

(Collapse in progress.) The pre-creases will help everything come together in the center. (See the next steps for reference.)

9

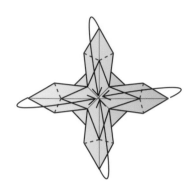

Fold the corners into the center using the existing pre-creases. (See the next step for reference.)

10

Flatten the model. This will create four squares on the top of the model. (Note: The next step is a magnified view.)

11

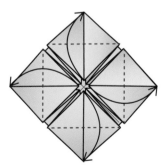

Fold the top corners to the back.

12

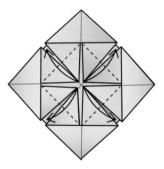

Fold the inner center corners out as well.

13

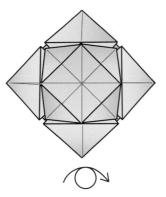

Turn the paper over.

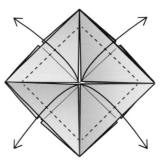

14

Fold the center corners out so they are slightly shorter than the full length. (See the next step for reference.)

15

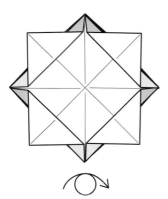

Turn the paper over.

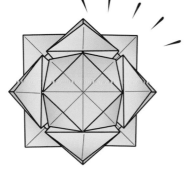

Enjoy your finished brooch!

BALLET FLATS

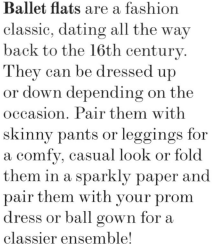

Ballet flats are a fashion classic, dating all the way back to the 16th century. They can be dressed up or down depending on the occasion. Pair them with skinny pants or leggings for a comfy, casual look or fold them in a sparkly paper and pair them with your prom dress or ball gown for a classier ensemble!

STYLE TIPS

- Ballet flats are the perfect choice if you're going to be on your feet; they're both comfortable and stylish!

- Toss a pair of ballet flats in your tote bag; they're easy to take on the go, and you'll be grateful to have them if your high heels start hurting!

How To Fold

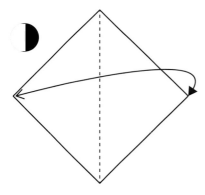

Fold the paper in half diagonally and then unfold. (Note: The side facing down will become the outside of the ballet flats.)

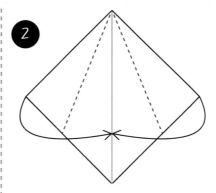

Fold the side edges into the center crease.

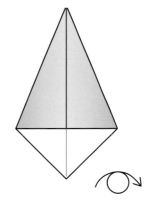

Turn the paper over.

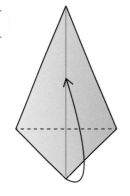

Fold the bottom triangle up at the lower edge of the side creases.

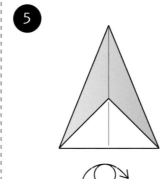

Turn the paper over.

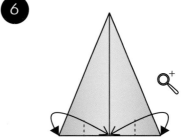

Pinch two reference points along the bottom edge by bringing both corners into the center crease and then unfold. (Note: The next step is a magnified view.)

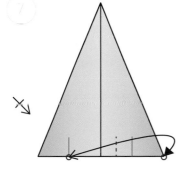

Pinch another reference crease by bringing the right corner across to the pinch on the left side and then unfold. Repeat on the opposite side.

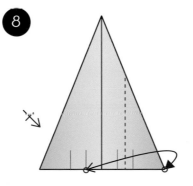

Fold the right corner across to the pinch closest to the center on the left side and then unfold. Repeat on the opposite side.

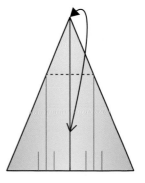

Fold the top corner down at the top edge of the creases made in the previous step and then unfold.

10

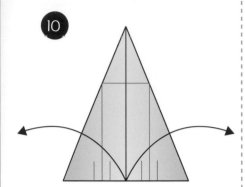

Open the flaps back
out to the sides.

11

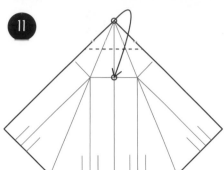

Fold the top corner down to
the crease made in step #9.

12

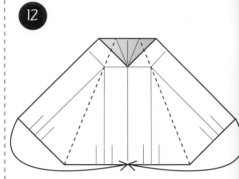

Fold the side flaps back into the
center on the existing pre-creases.

13

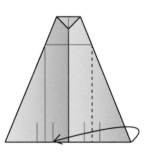

Fold the right side across
on the existing pre-crease
made in step #8.

14

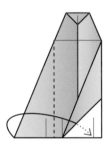
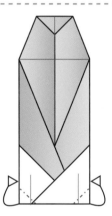

Fold the opposite side across
on the existing pre-crease
and insert it into the pocket of
the other flap. (Note: The next
step is a magnified view.)

15

Mountain fold the bottom
corners to the back to
shape the front of the shoe.

16

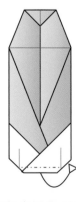

Mountain fold the bottom
edge to the back to further
shape the front of the shoe.

17

Fold the top section down
on the existing pre-crease.

18

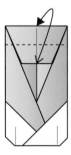

Fold the top edge down to the
bottom edge of the flap from the
previous step and then unfold.

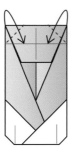

19

Fold the top corners down to line up with the crease made in the previous step.

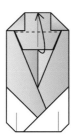

20

Fold the flap back up, hiding the folded corners from previous step. This will create a paper lock.

21

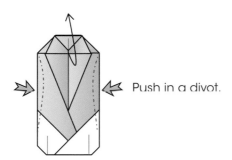

Push in a divot.

Gently lift the back section from inside the pocket to open and shape the shoe. (Note: Hold the paper lock you creased in the previous step while lifting the back up—the triangles need to remain locked underneath the flap.) Lift the sides and push them in slightly to further shape the shoe. This will make the shoe 3-D.

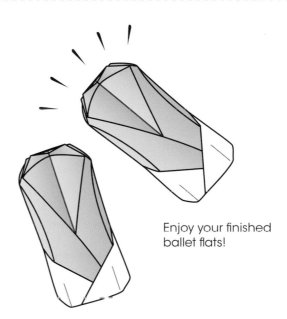

Enjoy your finished ballet flats!

*These instructions will make one finished ballet flat. Fold another one to make a pair! You can vary the shape of each model—creating a left and right shoe—by folding the corners in different sizes in step #15 and by shaping in step #21.)

BRACELET

Origami lends itself very easily to becoming jewelry. You can turn almost any origami model into pieces of jewelry that you can wear. This simple paper **bracelet** uses the same paper lock as a few of the other designs in this book. Try playing with proportions and different colors to make it your own accessory. Coordinate your bracelet with your other jewelry by choosing complementary colors, but don't make it too matchy-matchy.

HOW TO USE

- Try folding this bracelet in a variety of colors and patterns. Then stack several bracelets for a wrist full of fun bangles.

- Fold this model with smaller paper, and it can function as a ring instead of a bracelet.

How To Fold

1

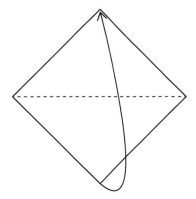

Fold the paper in half diagonally.

2

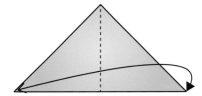

Fold the paper in half again and then unfold.

3

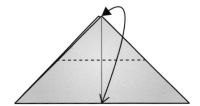

Fold the top corner (through both layers of paper) down to the bottom edge and then unfold.

4

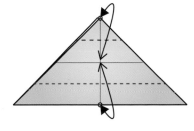

Fold both the top corner and bottom edge to the center crease and then unfold.

5

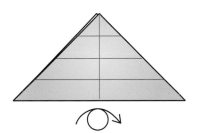

Turn the paper over.

6

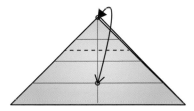

Fold the top corner down to the bottom crease made in step #4 and then unfold.

7

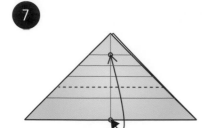

Fold the bottom edge up to the top crease made in step #4 and then unfold. (Note: You are dividing the paper diagonally into sixteenths.)

8

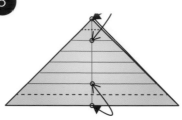

Fold the top corner down to the nearest crease and then unfold. Do the same with the bottom edge.

9

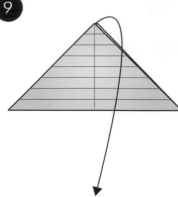

Open the paper back to the original square.

10

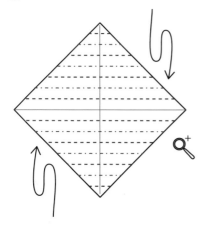

Working first from the top, then from the bottom, pleat the paper using the creases made in the previous steps. (Note: The top half will have all the creases going in the correct direction, but you will need to reverse the creases on the bottom half. See the next step—a magnified view—for reference.)

11

Fold the outer corners into the center crease.

12

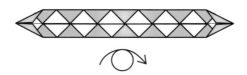

Turn the paper over.

13

Fold the outer corners into the center crease again and then unfold. (Note: This fold will involve only the back layers of paper, not the front layers.)

14

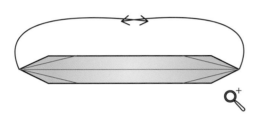

Wrap one corner around to the back and then insert it into the pocket on the opposite side. The pocket is the diagonal triangle flap folded in step #11. (Note: The next step is a magnified view.)

15

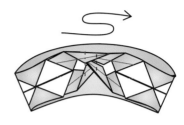

Pleat the back section where the corners overlap, creating a paper lock.

16

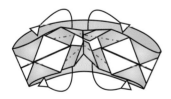

Mountain fold the paper to the inside along the diagonals folded in step #13 to complete the paper lock.

17

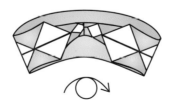

Turn the paper over.

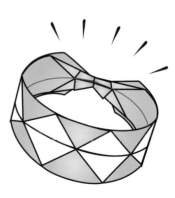

Enjoy your finished bracelet!

SUNGLASSES

Sunglasses are functional and can add unique flair to your style. Try folding these lenses into different shapes on the bottom. Don't forget to use different colors and patterns to coordinate your shades with a variety of outfits.

HOW TO USE

- Try folding these sunglasses out of clear or colored acetate to make your sunglasses functional and decorative.

- Don't forget to throw a pair of colorful shades in your tote bag—along with flip-flops!—for a day at the beach.

Pg. 44

How To Fold

1

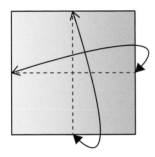

Fold the paper in half in both directions and then unfold. (Note: The side facing up will become the frame of the sunglasses; the side facing down will become the lenses.)

2

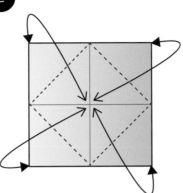

Fold all four corners into the center and then unfold.

3

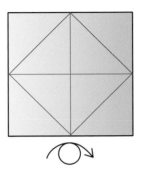

Turn the paper over.

4

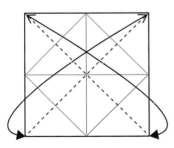

Fold the paper in half diagonally in both directions and then unfold.

5

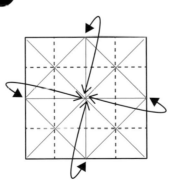

One at a time, fold all four side edges into the center crease and then unfold.

6

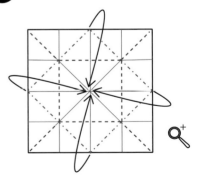

Fold each side of the square into the center at the same time while pinching the corners. (Note: The next step is a magnified view.)

7

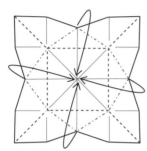

(Collapse in progress.) The existing pre-creases will help everything come together in the center.

8

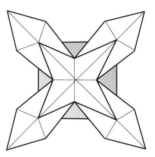

Collapse almost finished.

9

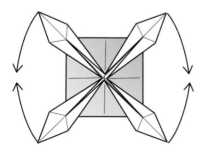

Fold the flaps down and in to make two trapezoid boat shapes. (See the next step for reference.)

10

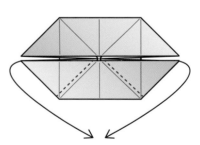

Fold the bottom corner flaps down so they don't quite meet in the center. The gap between the two sides will become the bridge of the glasses. (See the next step for reference.)

Fold the corners up and then
unfold. (Note: This is a new crease.)

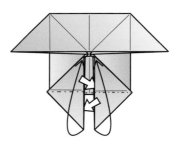

Open and squash the pockets on
the creases made in the previous
step to make flat squares.

Fold the upper corners down
to reveal the contrasting side
of the paper. This will become
the lenses of the sunglasses.

Fold the bottom corners up
and then unfold. There will still
be a small gap in the center.

15

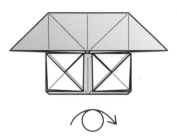

Turn the paper over.

16

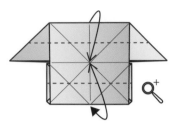

Fold the top and bottom edges into the center crease. Unfold only the bottom edge. (Note: The next step is a magnified view.)

17

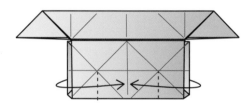

Fold the sides of the bottom section into the center and then unfold. (Note: This crease will be just a partial pinch and won't go all the way to the top.)

18

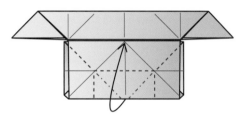

Bring the front layer of the bottom section up to the center and collapse using the pre-creases. These will help the bottom section lay flat. (See the next step for reference.)

19

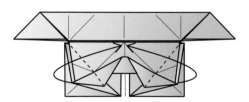

(Collapse in progress.) Push the blunted triangle section up along with the side corners and flatten. (See the next step for reference.)

20

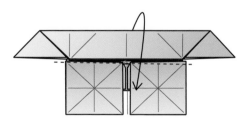

Fold down the top section.

Shape the lenses by folding in small corners on the bottom sections of each side. (Note: You can try different angles and shapes to give your sunglasses a different look.)

Fold the top section down and in half again. (Note: There are several layers of paper at the top. Fold all the layers together and press down to make a hard crease.)

Fold the sides in to make the arms of the glasses. (Note: You can also put a soft crease in the bridge of the glasses or a bend to shape the glasses and help the layers stay together.)

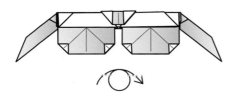

Turn the paper over.

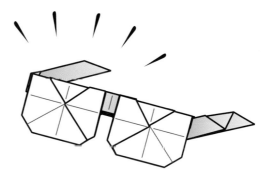

Enjoy your finished sunglasses!

CLUTCH

This easy-to-fold paper **clutch** was designed out of necessity. It's the perfect little pouch to hold all of your essentials for a night out—everything from a phone to lipstick to money. Fold in a sophisticated pattern and pair your clutch with a ball gown, prom dress, or little black dress.

HOW TO USE

⊞ Fold in a variety of papers to coordinate with an array of outfits.

⊞ Try folding the clutch using a paper-lined fabric, such as bookbinding paper, or a thicker card stock to make your own functional clutch.

How To Fold

1

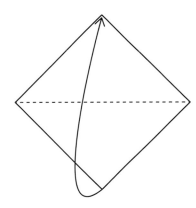

Fold the paper in half diagonally. (Note: The side facing down will become the outside of your clutch; the side facing up will be the lining.)

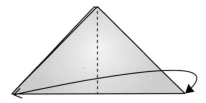

2

Fold the paper in half again and then unfold.

3

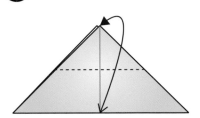

Using just the top layer of paper, fold the top corner down to the bottom edge and then unfold.

4

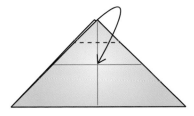

Still using just the top layer of paper, fold the top corner down to the crease made in the previous step.

5

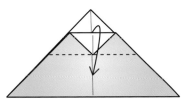

Fold the top layer down on the existing pre-crease.

6

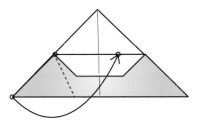

Fold the bottom left corner up and line it up along the folded edge. (Use the circled points for reference.)

7

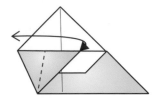

Using the bottom corner as a starting point, fold the top triangle in half and then unfold.

8

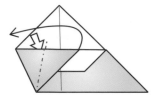

Open and squash fold the pocket on the existing pre-creases.

9

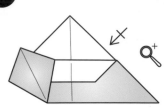

Repeat steps #6–8 on the opposite side. (Note: The next step is a magnified view.)

10

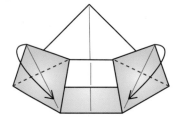

Fold the top triangle flaps down on each side.

11

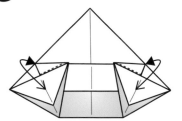

Fold the small triangle flaps still sticking out on top down and then unfold.

12

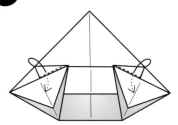

Tuck the small triangle flaps in. (Note: This is not an inside reverse. Just fold the flaps under the top layer to hold them in place.)

13

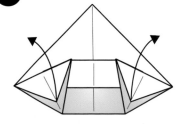

Unfold the front triangles back up to the top.

14

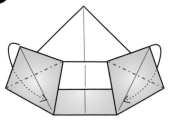

Mountain fold and tuck the flaps in on the existing pre-creases. (Note: This fold will cover up the paper lock made in step #12.) Don't tuck the triangles in between layers, just fold them to the back.

15

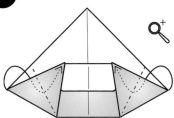

Inside reverse the outer corners on the existing pre-creases. (Note: The next step is a magnified view.)

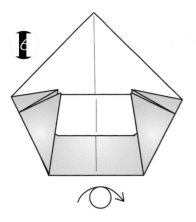

16

Turn the paper over.

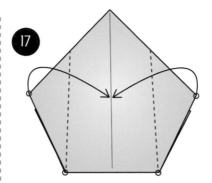

17

Fold the side corners into the center, using the circled points as a reference. Start your fold from the bottom corner and make the side corners touch and meet in the center.

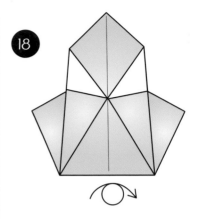

18

Turn the paper over.

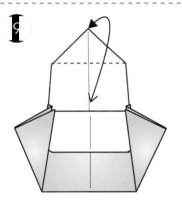

19

Fold the top triangle down and then unfold.

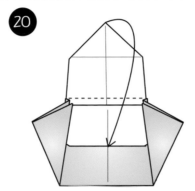

20

Fold the entire top flap down and over the front of the clutch.

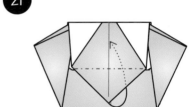

21

Mountain fold and tuck the small triangle under on the existing pre-crease to lock it in place. (You can also valley fold this triangle up and over the back to create a completely contrasting top pocket.)

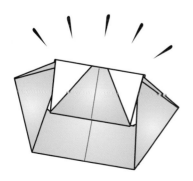

Enjoy your finished clutch!

Fold your clutch in a neutral pattern!

BACKPACK

Practical and modern, this geometric **backpack** uses a simple paper lock to make the straps. A backpack can be used as a functional school accessory or in place of a purse to hold your belongings and keep you looking smart and stylish.

STYLE TIPS

- Pair with jeans or skinny pants and an easy top—like a T-shirt or sweater—for a casual look.

- Backpacks make great travel bags—just throw yours over your shoulder and go!

How To Fold

1

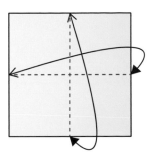

Fold the paper in half in both directions and then unfold. (Note: The side facing up will become the pattern of the backpack.)

2

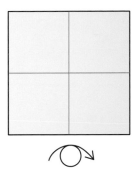

Turn the paper over.

3

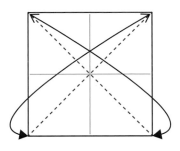

Fold the paper in half diagonally in both directions and then unfold.

4

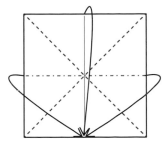

Bring the sides and top down to the bottom to collapse into a triangle with four loose flaps on the bottom. (See the next step for reference.)

5

Using just the top layer, fold the side edges into the center crease.

6

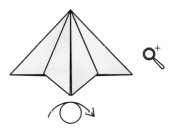

Turn the paper over. (Note: The next step is a magnified view.)

7

Fold the top corner down to the bottom edge and then unfold.

8

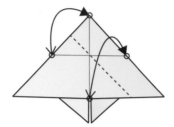

Fold the top corner down to the left edge (to the start of the crease made in the previous step) and then unfold. (Note: This diagonal fold will go through the center of the creases.)

9

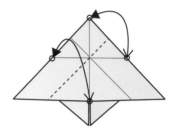

Repeat step #8 in the other direction and then unfold.

10

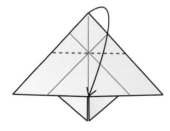

Fold the top corner down on the existing pre-crease.

11

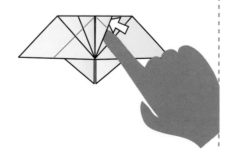

Find the pocket to the right of the center triangle. (Note: This is to help with the steps #12 and 13.)

12

Using the pre-crease made in step #8, fold the flap down on the inside of the pocket.

 13

 14

 15

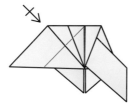

Fold in progress. (Note: Make sure to go all the way to the inside corner of the pocket to make this fold.)

Repeat steps #11–13 on the opposite side.

Turn the paper over.

 16

 17

18

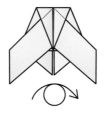

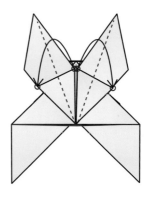

Fold the bottom center flaps up to the top and out to the sides as far as the paper will allow. (See the next step for reference.)

Fold the circled points into the center crease. The corners won't quite reach the top on this fold. (Note: The next step is a magnified view.)

Narrow the flaps by folding in half. Use the circled points for reference.

19

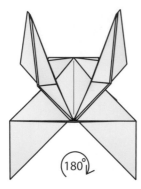

Rotate the paper 180°.

20

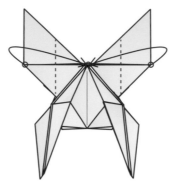

Fold the sides of the new top section into the center.

21

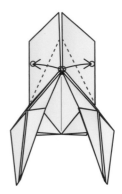

Fold the center corners toward the sides, making sure they don't quite reach the edges. (Note: This will create a pocket for the lower half of the backpack strap, locking the top and bottom straps together.)

22

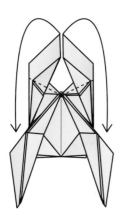

Fold the top flaps to the front, lining up the side edges so they are as perpendicular as possible. (See the next step for reference.)

23

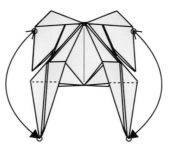

Fold the bottom flaps up to line up with the outside edges of the top flaps and then unfold. The side edges should align and be as parallel as possible to the center vertical line. (See the next step for reference.)

24

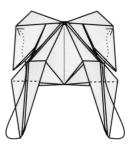

Using the existing pre-crease, insert the bottom flaps into the openings at the bottom of the top flaps.

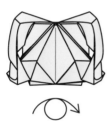

Fold the side edges to narrow the straps.

Holding the straps together in the center so they don't slip, gently pull and round the straps to shape the backpack. (Note: You can narrow the straps further to make a stronger paper lock.)

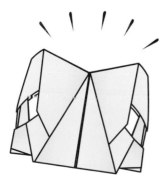

Turn the paper over.

Enjoy your finished backpack!

Fold your backpack in unexpected patterns!

FLIP-FLOPS

Flip-flops are easy to wear and carry, which makes them an essential accessory during the warm summer months. Just throw them in your bag and go! Try folding this paper version with large newspaper to make a life-sized pair of flip-flops.

STYLE TIPS

- Flip-flops are a must with a swimsuit at the beach in the summer.

- Pair your flip-flops with shorts and a T-shirt, or with a romper for an easy summer look.

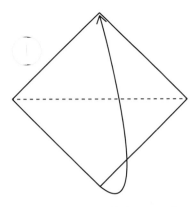

1. Fold paper in half diagonally. (Note: The side facing down will become the color/pattern of your flip-flop.)

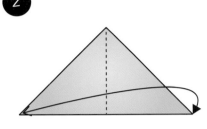

2. Fold the paper in half horizontally and then unfold.

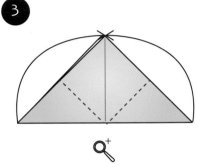

3. Fold the bottom corners up to the top. (Note: The next step is a magnified view.)

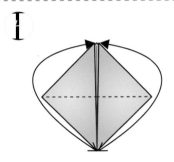

4. Fold the top corners down to the bottom and then unfold.

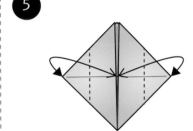

5. Fold the side corners into the center and then unfold.

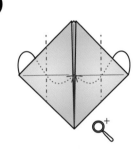

6. Inside reverse the corners on the crease created in the previous step. (Note: The next step is a magnified view.)

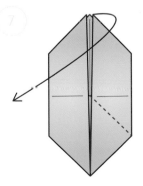

7. Fold the right corner flap down and across.

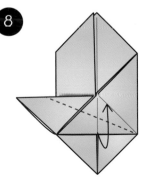

8. Fold the bottom edge of the flap up to the pre-existing diagonal crease. (See the next step for reference.)

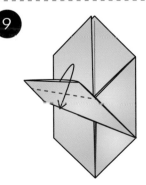

9. Fold the top edge of the flap down to line up with the folded diagonal edge. (See the next step for reference.)

10

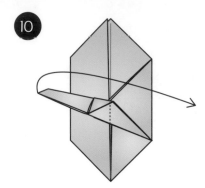

Fold the flap back out to the side along the center crease. (See the next step for reference.)

11

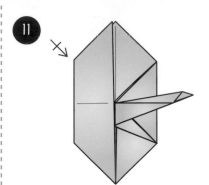

Repeat steps #7–10 on the opposite side.

12

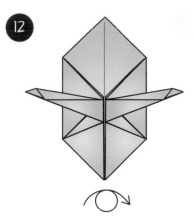

Turn the paper over.

13

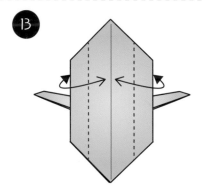

Fold the sides in so they don't quite meet in the center and then unfold. This will determine the width of the flip-flop.

14

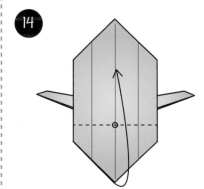

Fold the bottom edge up. Use the point where the side flaps meet in the center on the opposite side as a reference.

15

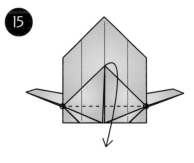

Fold the top corner back down at the indicated points.

16

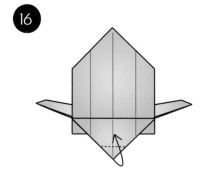

Fold the bottom corner up to blunt and shape the front of the flip-flop.

17

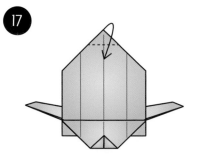

Fold the top corner down as well to blunt and shape the back of the flip-flop.

18

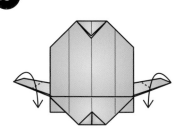

Fold the side flaps down at about the halfway point at an approximately 90° angle. (See the next step for reference.)

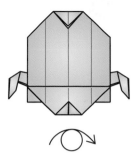

Turn the paper over.

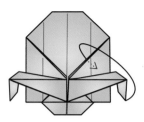

Lift one side flap and slide it underneath the diagonal edge. The tip you folded in step #18 will slide under but needs to line up with the vertical pre-crease from step #13. (Note: The model will become 3-D at this point as you create the straps.)

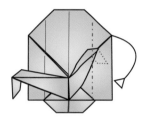

Mountain fold the side edge to the back, locking the tip of the flap in place and creating one of the flip-flop straps.

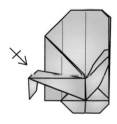

Repeat steps #20–21 on the opposite side. (Note: There are several layers to fold to the back. Push hard and flatten before you gently round and shape the straps.)

Enjoy your finished flip-flop!

*These instructions will make one finished flip-flop. Fold another to make a pair.

About The Author

Sok Song's passion for folding paper bloomed from a hobby he taught himself during childhood into an award-winning origami-design business called Creased, Inc. He later attended Parsons with the intention of incorporating his origami skills into garment construction and fashion design. Sok's work has been featured on numerous TV shows, including *America's Next Top Model* and *Extreme Home Makeover*. His work has also been included in magazines such as *Cosmopolitan*, *Elle*, *GQ*, *Harper's Bazaar*, *Icon*, *InStyle*, *Marie Claire*, *Pop*, *Self*, *Vanity Fair*, and *Vogue*. Other notable clients include Condé Nast Publications Ltd., Harrods, Macy's, Saks Fifth Avenue, The Museum of Art and Design, The American Museum of Natural History, and *The New Yorker*. Sok currently lives in New York City, although his folding work takes him all over the world.

Read More

Arcturus Publishing. *Fashion Origami*. London, England: Arcturus Publishing Limited, 2014.

Song, Sok. *Everyday Origami: A Foldable Fashion Guide*. Fashion Origami. North Mankato, Minn.: Capstone Press, 2016.

Savvy is published by Capstone Press
A Capstone Imprint
1710 Roe Crest Drive
North Mankato, Minnesota 56003
www.mycapstone.com

Designs, illustrations, and text © Sok Song 2016
Photographs © Capstone 2016

Library of Congress Cataloging-in-Publication Data is available on the Library of Congress website.

ISBN: 978-1-5157-1623-5 (library binding) — 978-1-5157-1646-4 (ebook PDF)

Summary: Ten original fashion origami accessories complete with written instructions and illustrated diagrams.

Editor: Alison Deering
Designer: Aruna Rangarajan

Image Credits: Photographs by Capstone Studio: Karon Dubke, Sarah Schuette, studio stylist; Marcy Morin, studio scheduler; Author photo by Alexanda Grablewski
Folding Paper textures: Shutterstock: Alex Gontar, Love_Kay, maralova, Mirinka, MotionLight, OJardin, Ola-la, Olga Lebedeva, Prezoom.nl, Regina Jershova, tukkki, Vikpit, wacomka, WorkingPENS
Design Elements: Shutterstock: Altana8, Baksiabat, BeatWalk, Iveta Angelova, Lyubov, Lomonos, Nadin3d, OJardin, Transia Design, Zubada

Printed and bound in the USA.   009684F16